# LONG LOAN

ied

# RAINFOREST DESTRUCTION

© Aladdin Books Ltd 1990

Designed and produced by
Aladdin Books Ltd
28 Percy Street
London W1P 9FF

First published in
Great Britain in 1990 by
Franklin Watts Ltd
96 Leonard Street
London EC2A 4RH

ISBN 0 7496 0199 X

A CIP catalogue record for this
book is available from the British
Library.

Printed in Belgium

The publishers would like to
acknowledge that the
photographs reproduced within
this book have been posed by
models or have been obtained
from photographic agencies.

| | |
|---|---|
| Design | David West Children's Book Design |
| Editor | Elise Bradbury |
| Picture research | Cecilia Weston-Baker |
| Illustrator | Ian Moores |

The author, Dr Tony Hare, is a
writer, ecologist and TV
presenter. He works with several
environmental organisations
including the London Wildlife
Trust, the British Association of
Nature Conservationists, and
Plantlife, of which he is Chairman
of the Board.

The consultants: Jacky Karas is a
Senior Research Associate at the
Climatic Research Unit at the
University of East Anglia.

Koy Thomson, formerly
international rainforest
campaigner for Friends of the
Earth, is now responsible for
Northern NGO liaison at the
International Institute for
Environment and Development.

**SAVE OUR EARTH**

# RAINFOREST DESTRUCTION

## TONY HARE

**GLOUCESTER PRESS**

London · New York · Toronto · Sydney

# CONTENTS

# INTRODUCTION

The world's tropical rainforests lie in a hot, wet belt across the Equator. They have existed for millions of years and contain many resources. They are one of the Earth's most valuable possessions.

In them live over half the world's species of plants and animals. They also provide us with many types of food and medicine. Rainforests are a beautiful, noisy, colourful treasury of life where native peoples have lived in harmony with their environment for generations. All of us rely on rainforests; they absorb a lot of carbon dioxide ($CO_2$), keeping the gases in the atmosphere in balance. If rainforests are burned down, so releasing the absorbed $CO_2$, the world's climate could warm considerably, (known as global warming), because $CO_2$ traps heat in the atmosphere.

Yet we continue to clear the rainforests, destroying people's homes, potential food and drugs for the future, and the habitats of many plants and animals. Nameless species are made extinct before we have even seen, researched or understood them.

◄ **Tropical rainforests, like this one in El Salvador, form one of the richest and most varied habitats on Earth. Yet we are destroying them for farming, ranching and timber. The cleared area in this rainforest will be used for farming. Since the 1940s half of the world's tropical rainforest has been destroyed.**

# WHAT IS A RAINFOREST?

Many types of life thrive in the humid conditions of a rainforest, but trees dominate. From the air the forest is like a huge green carpet, with the tops of the trees forming a canopy which covers all traces of earth. In and beneath the canopy is an amazingly complex world. There are plants of all shapes and sizes growing everywhere – including all over the trees themselves. Among the plants live the many rainforest animals.

Rainforests exist in the tropics where it regularly rains. The dense forest vegetation keeps the air hot and humid. Everything is recycled and in balance within the rainforest. Some of the rainwater passes from the canopy down to the roots and then up through the tree to the air above, only to fall again as rain on another part of the forest. Some rainforests have stayed in this state of balance for 60 million years, and during this time the great variety of rainforest life has evolved.

▼ **This Costa Rican tropical rainforest is similar in many ways to the woodlands of Europe and North America. Both consist mainly of trees. But our forests are not hot and wet, and the plants and animals they support are very different.**

# THE RAINFOREST

The trees in a tropical rainforest are of many different species, and the top branches of the highest trees form a continuous canopy up to 50m above the ground. Above the canopy rise some taller trees known as emergents. The dense canopy is fully exposed to the bright sun, but the ground below is dimly lit, with the trunks of the trees towering high above. Some plants grow on the forest floor, others climb the trunks of the trees. Smaller trees grow below the main canopy. They form a lower layer, known as the sub-canopy, which is often hard to distinguish.

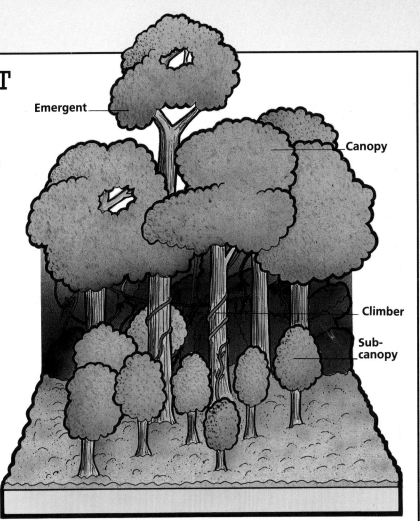

Emergent

Canopy

Climber

Sub-canopy

# WHERE ARE THEY?

The world's hot lands lie in a great band around the tropics, on either side of the Equator. Where these areas are wet as well as warm – where rain-heavy air sweeps in year-round off the oceans to fall on the land – the world's tropical rainforests grow.

At one time these rainforests covered huge areas of Africa, South and Central America, Asia and the Pacific Islands. However, in recent decades they have been destroyed at an alarming rate. By 1980 nearly half of the rainforests that existed on the Earth at the beginning of the century had been destroyed. In 1989, 1.8 per cent of the world's remaining rainforests were destroyed, and the rate of destruction increased by 90 per cent between 1979-89. In the last 30 years Central America has lost over half of its rainforests.

▼ **The largest remaining tropical rainforest lies around the River Amazon and its tributaries in Brazil, Venezuela and Peru.**

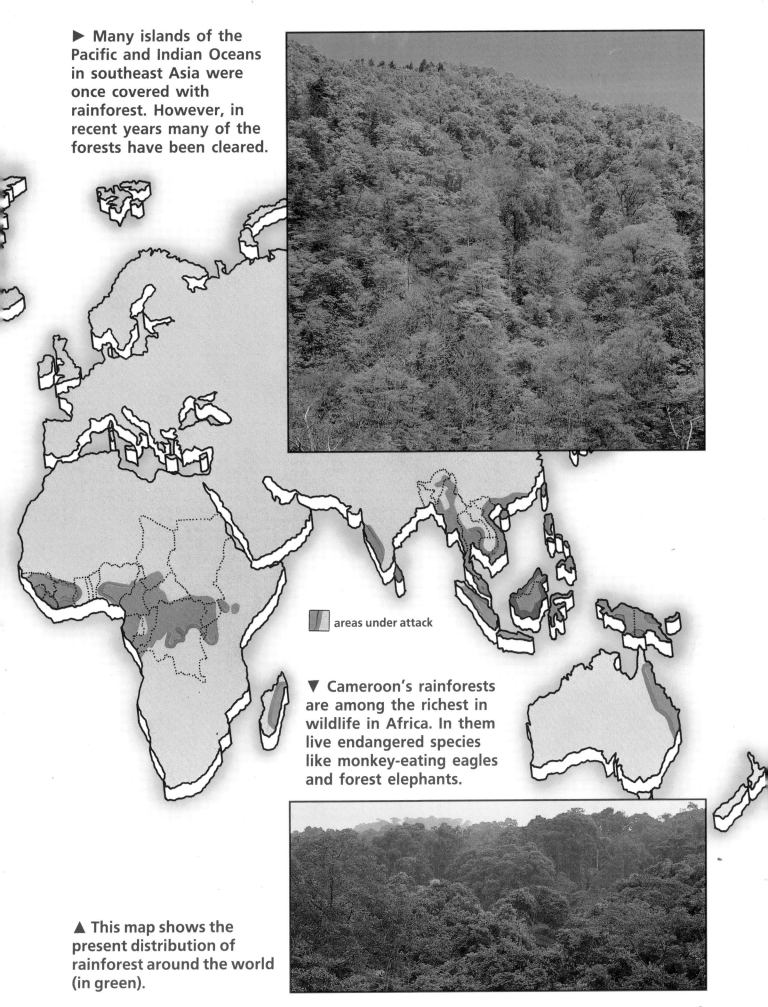

▶ Many islands of the Pacific and Indian Oceans in southeast Asia were once covered with rainforest. However, in recent years many of the forests have been cleared.

areas under attack

▼ Cameroon's rainforests are among the richest in wildlife in Africa. In them live endangered species like monkey-eating eagles and forest elephants.

▲ This map shows the present distribution of rainforest around the world (in green).

# RAINFOREST DESTRUCTION

The reason why the rainforests now cover only a portion of the area which they did in the past is because they have been destroyed by people. Every day huge areas of rainforest disappear, particularly in the Amazon and southeast Asia, as the trees are felled, bulldozed, or burned down.

Many temperate forests (forests which grow in moderate climates, with no huge extremes in temperature or rainfall) in North America, Europe and Asia have been felled over the ages for farming and settling, leaving the tropical rainforests as the last great treelands on Earth. The clearing of the temperate forests was done gradually, but the rainforests can now be cleared at a frightening rate: with a chainsaw, felling a tree can be done in minutes.

The rainforests are rich in plants and animals, many of which occur in just one tiny patch of forest. Some scientists estimate that as many as one species every half hour is made extinct by rainforest clearing.

▼ The fires raging through the tropical rainforests are so huge that they can be easily picked out from space by satellites, as can the clearings made in the Brazilian Amazon. On either side of a highway cut through a rainforest lies some 19 km of destruction.

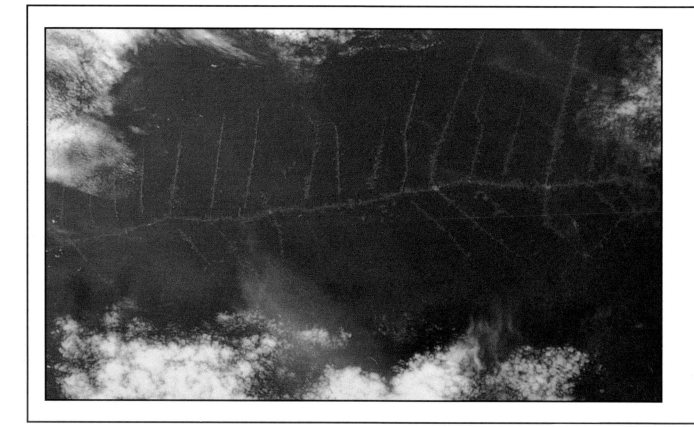

► **Every minute an average of 100 acres of rainforest, which is equivalent to about 60 football pitches, is lost. Over a year this amounts to an area the size of England, Scotland and Wales being destroyed.**

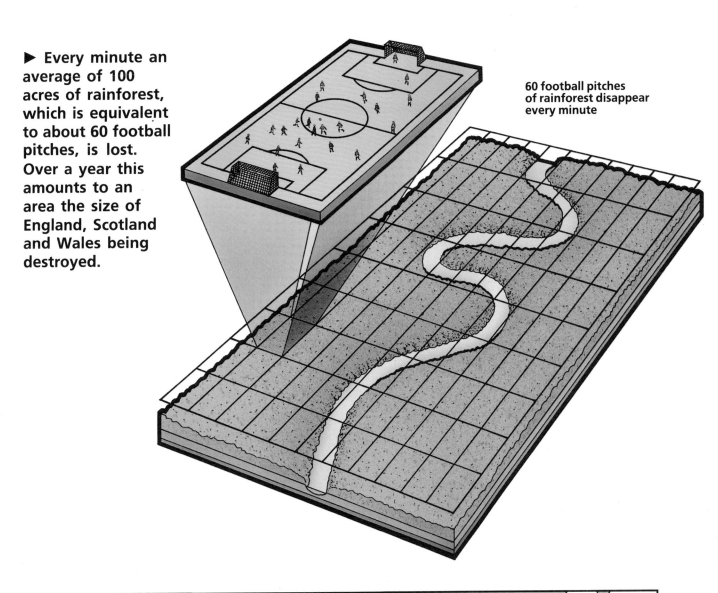

60 football pitches of rainforest disappear every minute

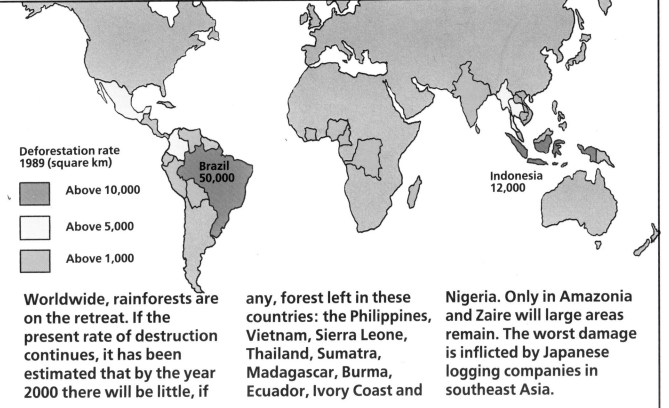

**Deforestation rate 1989 (square km)**

Above 10,000

Above 5,000

Above 1,000

**Brazil 50,000**

**Indonesia 12,000**

**Worldwide, rainforests are on the retreat. If the present rate of destruction continues, it has been estimated that by the year 2000 there will be little, if** **any, forest left in these countries: the Philippines, Vietnam, Sierra Leone, Thailand, Sumatra, Madagascar, Burma, Ecuador, Ivory Coast and** **Nigeria. Only in Amazonia and Zaire will large areas remain. The worst damage is inflicted by Japanese logging companies in southeast Asia.**

# WHY IS IT HAPPENING?

Money and survival are the two main reasons why people are destroying the rainforests. Some people fell the forests to make large profits, while others clear them because it is the only way for them to survive.

Some forest land is cleared for mining minerals which lie beneath the ground. Other land is cleared for cattle ranching, or to be replaced by eucalyptus plantations for the paper pulp industry. Also, many tropical trees are felled for their timber.

In many parts of the tropics poverty is the reason for rainforest destruction. People are forced to move into the forests to scratch a living because there is nowhere else for them to go. They chop down and burn the forest, and plant their crops in the cleared ground. Rainforest soils are not very fertile, and after a few years of intense cultivation all the nutrients in the soil are used up. The people have to move on to a new patch of forest. This is called "shifted cultivation" or "slash and burn".

▼ **Eucalyptus plantations can bring greenery back to devastated rainforest areas. Yet in many countries rainforest has been cleared in order to plant eucalyptus. It is grown for paper pulp, but it also drains nutrients and water from the soil.**

▼ Tropical woods like mahogany and teak are often used for furniture and other objects. Usually the timber is obtained with no thought for the forest. When loggers fell a tree for its timber, the surrounding forest is damaged by the loggers and their bulldozers.

▲ Many of Brazil's cattle live on ranches which were once rainforest. Forests are burned and replaced with grass for the cattle; some end up as hamburgers.

◄► Parts of rainforests are remote and difficult for settlers to reach until roads are driven through. Roads are made by governments improving transport, and by loggers exploiting new areas for timber. People who have nowhere else to go follow the new roads to cultivate the land before moving on. Their method of farming, called shifted cultivation, saps the nutrients from the soil and destroys the surrounding forest so it cannot grow back. The impact on the forest grows as more people move into it.

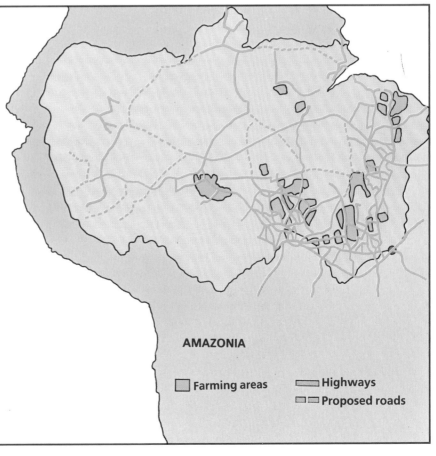

AMAZONIA

☐ Farming areas     ▭ Highways
                             ▭▭ Proposed roads

# PARADISE LOST

Because the temperature of the rainforest stays fairly constant, life reproduces all year round. Tropical rainforests are home to at least half of the species of plants and animals in the world although they occupy only seven per cent of the Earth's land surface. They teem with life, from the ground all the way up to the canopy. Animals and plants of all kinds live in the forests, from ants to jaguars, and from the mighty emergent trees to the tiniest fungi.

A rainforest is a web of life. Trees are covered with other plants; some of them are climbers, which twist and turn around the tree's trunk. Other plants find rootholds among the branches. Among the plants live the animals. Some are leaf-eaters like sloths and monkeys, while others are hunters, like the anteater searching out ants, and big cats like tigers hunting larger prey.

Many of the forest animals live in the canopy, and are more often heard than seen. The forest is a very noisy place, especially at night. Along with the drumming of the rain, the air is full of the buzz of insects, the howls of monkeys, the croaks of frogs and the calls of birds.

▼ **(From left to right),** *toucans* **are typical rainforest birds of South American forest canopies.** *Insects* **(this one is a frangipani caterpillar from Panama) abound in all rainforests, but** *lemurs* **live only in Madagascar's rainforests. This** *3-toed sloth* **mother with young lives in South and Central American rainforests, and** *gorillas* **inhabit Africa's rainforests.**

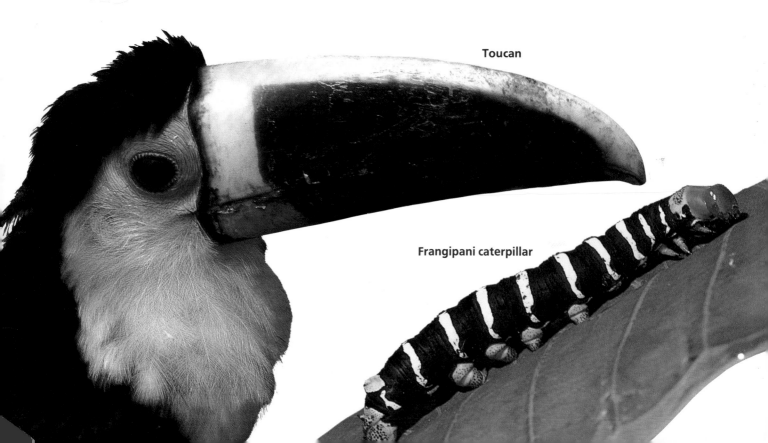

Toucan

Frangipani caterpillar

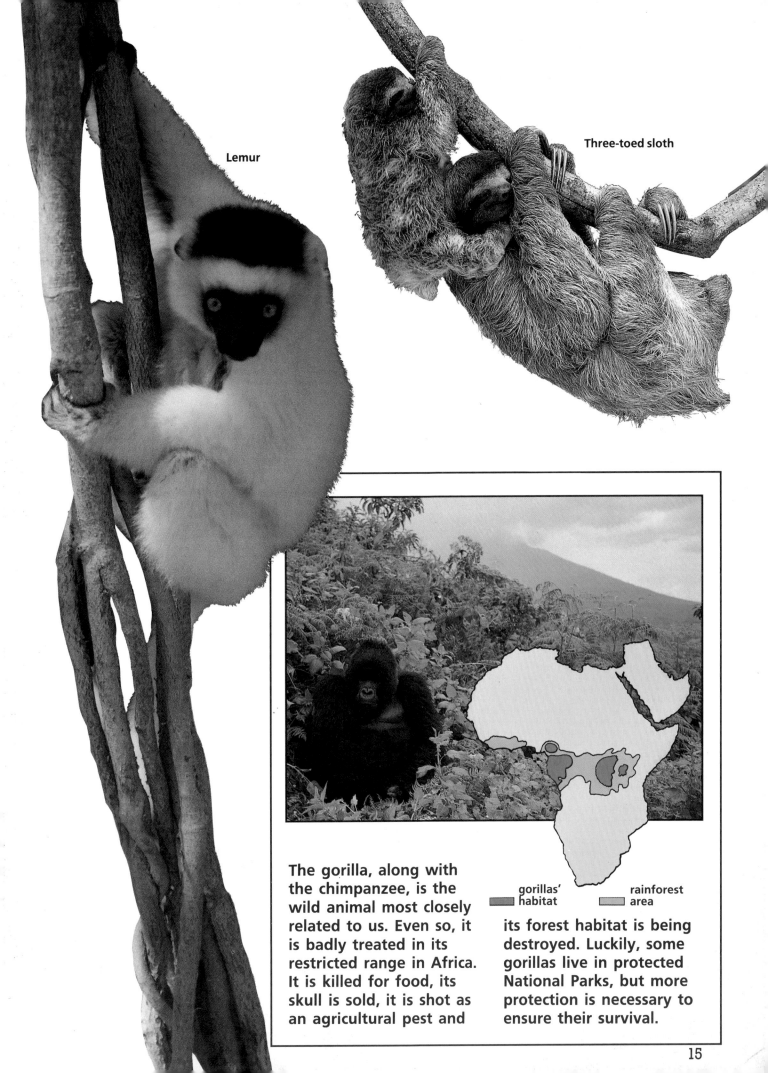

Lemur

Three-toed sloth

gorillas' habitat

rainforest area

The gorilla, along with the chimpanzee, is the wild animal most closely related to us. Even so, it is badly treated in its restricted range in Africa. It is killed for food, its skull is sold, it is shot as an agricultural pest and its forest habitat is being destroyed. Luckily, some gorillas live in protected National Parks, but more protection is necessary to ensure their survival.

# RAINFOREST MEDICINES

Some of the plants of the rainforests have proved to be of great importance to people because they provide vital medicines. At least a quarter of the world's most important medicines are based on rainforest plants. The variety of treatments from these tropical products includes painkillers, cough mixtures, drugs that relieve anxiety, birth-control pills, anaesthetics, antibiotics and cancer-fighting drugs.

Only one per cent of tropical plants have yet been carefully tested for their potential as medicines. Some scientists believe that as high as ten per cent of untested plants may have the potential to fight cancer. Also, a species of tree found in the Amazon and Australia contains a substance which is being researched in London as a possible treatment for AIDS.

▼▶ **The following rainforest plants provide medicines for illnesses: the rosy periwinkle of Madagascar for leukaemia; the calabar bean of West Africa for eye disorders; and the papaya of Latin America for stomach illnesses.**

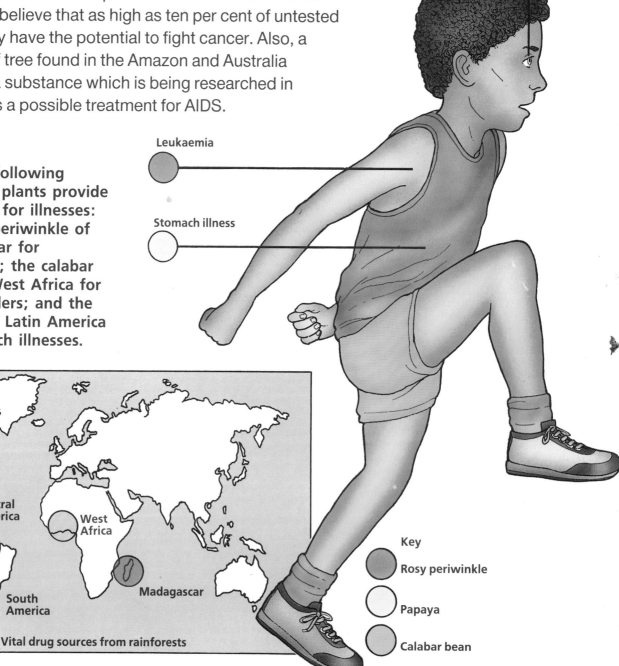

Eye disorders

Leukaemia

Stomach illness

Central America

West Africa

South America

Madagascar

Vital drug sources from rainforests

Key

Rosy periwinkle

Papaya

Calabar bean

◀ Many food crops that originally came from the rainforests are now grown in plantations rather than harvested wild in the jungle. But domestic crops still need their wild relatives. Wild plants often have qualities which cultivated varieties lack, like especially good flavour or disease resistance. People, like this botanist, search for the plants' relatives in the forests so they can introduce their qualities to the cultivated crops by cross-breeding them.

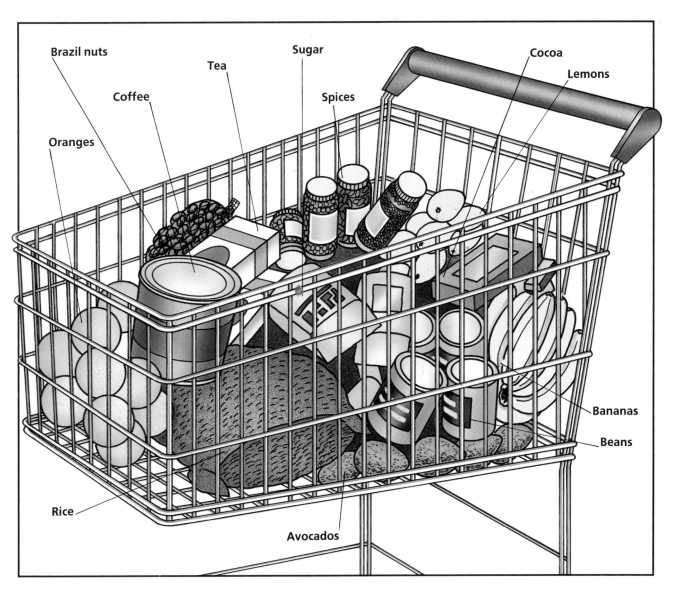

Brazil nuts

Sugar

Cocoa

Lemons

Tea

Coffee

Spices

Oranges

Bananas

Beans

Rice

Avocados

# DEFORESTATION EFFECTS

Scientists warn that large-scale rainforest destruction could have devastating effects upon life on our planet. Burning the rainforests releases gases into the atmosphere which add to the greenhouse effect. This process, in which heat is trapped in the atmosphere by certain gases like $CO_2$, threatens to raise the Earth's temperature, with potentially disastrous results.

Another serious impact of the destruction is that the removal of rainforests leaves behind bare earth. In hilly areas this means that large amounts of water run off the land instead of being trapped by the forests, so soil is washed away and floods occur. Flooding of this type has occurred in many places, like Madagascar and the Philippines. Disastrous floods, caused by forest destruction, led Thailand to ban all logging in 1989.

**Rainforest plants, like other plants, take up carbon dioxide ($CO_2$) from the atmosphere and turn it into substances that are vital for growth and life. But when they are burned the $CO_2$ is released again. Carbon dioxide is a "greenhouse gas" and it adds to the greenhouse effect, helping to cause global warming which threatens to disrupt the climate worldwide. Over a billion tonnes of $CO_2$ are estimated to be released from rainforest burning every year; this is second only to the amount released from burning coal, oil and gas in contributing to global warming.**

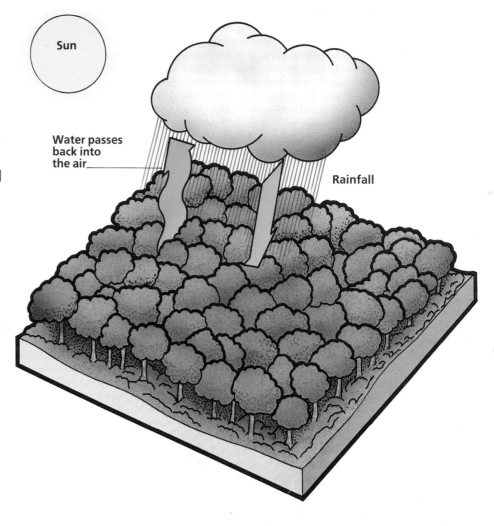

Sun

Water passes back into the air

Rainfall

Native forest people sometimes clear patches of forest to grow crops, but do no lasting harm. They choose a small area of forest (1), clear and burn it (2), grow carefully chosen crops (3), continue to grow different crops over a few years (4), farming the land carefully and not intensively, then (5), leave the forest to grow back. The unharmed forest that surrounds the clearing spreads out to cover the gap. Many years later the same patch of forest may be used again. This is called "shifting cultivation".

1.

2.

3.

4.

5.

# WHAT CAN BE DONE?

Saving the rainforests is a difficult problem, but it can be done. It demands a major effort by the countries of the world working together to make sure that the forests remain a habitat for millions of animals and plants, a source of food and medicines for the future and a home to tribal peoples.

One of the most important priorities lies in educating people all over the world about the value of the rainforests and the precious resources they hold. We must ensure that the governments in countries with rainforests become committed to saving them. Other countries have to help and, if necessary, give economic support to the rainforest countries.

For the rainforests to survive they must have complete protection in National Parks where possible, and sustainable use, instead of overexploitation, of unprotected forests. This is possible if the rainforest peoples are allowed to protect and manage their own forests. The global consequences will be disastrous if the current rate of destruction is not slowed.

Huge organisations, like the World Bank, and rich Western countries help to fund development schemes such as roads and dams in the tropics. Sometimes these schemes benefit the people in the area, but not always. Some projects, like roads through the Amazon, can do more harm than good. Now the World Bank is beginning to look at the environmental effects of such schemes before it supports them.

► Rubber is collected by cutting grooves in the bark of the rubber tree so that the latex (raw rubber) runs down into a cup. Although there are human-made rubber substitutes, none of them are as elastic or heat-resistant as the natural product. Rubber is particularly useful in tyres because it enables them to withstand potholes and emergency stops. This rubber is being collected at a Malaysian plantation, but rubber tapping in the wild is preferable because some rainforests are cleared for rubber tree plantations.

◄ It is possible for people who live in rainforests to use the land in non-destructive ways. These Kenyan women are planting trees to ensure soil protection in the future. Trees shelter soil from the rain thus preventing it from being washed away. They also provide building materials and firewood, fruit and nuts for food, and rubber and other substances for industry. Trees live for many years and, if species compatible with the habitat are used, they do not exhaust the soil as other crops do. This means that people do not have to keep moving on and clearing new areas of forest. Useful trees can be planted within the rainforest, or grown in areas where rainforest has been cleared.

# WHAT YOU CAN DO

Worldwide government action is needed to save the rainforests, but there are also plenty of things that you and your school can do:

● Write to your MP showing your concern.
● Don't buy items made of tropical timbers taken carelessly from the forests (**Friends of the Earth** produces a guide to the right woods to use).
● Don't buy an exotic plant or animal, such as an orchid or a parrot, if it was collected in the wild.
● Write to these organisations for more information.

## Useful addresses:

**Friends of the Earth**
26-28 Underwood Street
LONDON N1 7JQ
*Tel: 071-490 1555*

**Living Earth**
10 Upper Grosvenor Street
LONDON W1X 9PA
*Tel: 071-499 0854*

**Rainforest Foundation**
5 Fitzroy Lodge
The Grove
Highgate
LONDON N6 5JU
*Tel: 081-348 2926*
071 4987603

**Survival International**
310 Edgware Road
LONDON W2 1DY
*Tel: 071-723 5535*

**WWF (Worldwide Fund for Nature)**
Panda House
Weyside Park
Catteshall Lane
GODALMING
Surrey GU7 1XR
*Tel: 0483 426444*

## Designing a poster:

One of the most important things that can be done is to make more people aware of the destruction of rainforests. One way you can do this is to make a poster to hang up on a school notice board.

1) Think up a striking or clever heading for the poster which will grab the attention of the viewers.

2) Design an illustration or symbol like the one shown here or cut pictures out of magazines and make a montage that conveys the main message.

3) Read through this book and try to summarise in about 30 – 40 words what rainforest destruction is all about and why it is a problem.

4) Again by reading through the book make some suggestions as to what can be done to prevent further destruction of the world's rainforests.

5) Include some other information if there is room; such as useful addresses to contact for more information or campaign material.

# SAVE THE RAINFORESTS

WE ARE CLEARING THE WORLD'S RAINFORESTS AT A RAPID RATE, LEADING TO AN INCREASE OF CARBON DIOXIDE WHICH MIGHT AFFECT THE GLOBAL CLIMATE. MANY PLANTS AND ANIMALS ARE MADE EXTINCT BY THIS DESTRUCTION WHICH AFFECTS US ALL!

## WHAT CAN YOU DO?

• EDUCATE PEOPLE ABOUT THE GREAT VALUE OF THE RAINFORESTS, AND EMPHASISE THE GLOBAL PROBLEMS DESTROYING THEM WILL CAUSE.

• DON'T BUY EXOTIC PLANTS OR ANIMALS OR ITEMS MADE FROM TROPICAL TIMBER.

• WRITE TO ORGANIZATIONS INVOLVED IN SAVING THE RAINFORESTS FOR MORE INFORMATION.

USEFUL ADDRESSES

# FACT FILE 1

### Temperate rainforests

There are some rainforests outside the tropics. In temperate lands where there is a great deal of rain, and where the weather is mild, with few or no frosts, temperate rainforests grow. In southeast Australia and Tasmania there are temperate rainforests, like those below in New South Wales, where eucalyptus trees and tree ferns flourish. Australia also contains tropical rainforests.

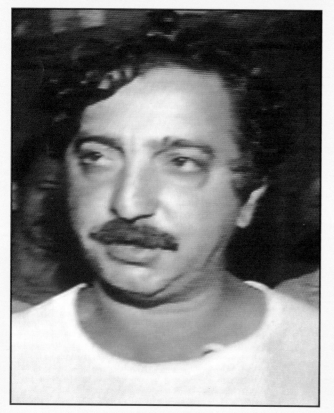

### Chico Mendes

Chico Mendes was a rubber tapper in the Amazon jungle. The rubber tappers collect or "tap" rubber from the rubber trees that grow wild in the forest; they exploit the forest's resources in a sustainable way. Mendes and the other rubber tappers resisted the attempts by wealthy landowners in Brazil to clear away the forests for ranching land. The Amazonian Indians supported and joined Mendes and others in the rubber tappers' union to try to save the forest. But Mendes' non-violent struggle earned him many enemies among those who destroy the forest and exploit its riches. On 22 December 1988 Mendes was shot dead by his enemies. Even though he has gone, the Indians and the rubber tappers will not give up. At Chico Mendes' funeral a banner was carried that read "They killed our leader, but not our struggle".

## Rainforest climate

Tropical rainforests thrive where the temperature is fairly constant all year at about 18-30°C (64-86°F) and where rain falls fairly regularly throughout the year. Rainforests get at least 200-300 cm (80-120 in) of rain a year, and some get as much as 1,000 cm (250 in). The climate never fluctuates to extremes like cold or drought. Nottingham, England, by comparison, has an average annual temperature of about 9.1°C (48°F) and an annual rainfall of about 71 cm (28 in), which does not fall regularly through the year.

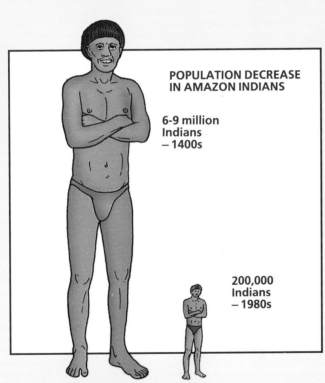

POPULATION DECREASE IN AMAZON INDIANS

6-9 million Indians – 1400s

200,000 Indians – 1980s

## Amazon Indians

The destruction of the rainforests and the diseases brought in by people from other places have drastically reduced the number of native people in the rainforests. In the Amazon, there were probably between 6 and 9 million Indians in the 1400s. Now there are only about 200,000, and they are threatened on all sides.

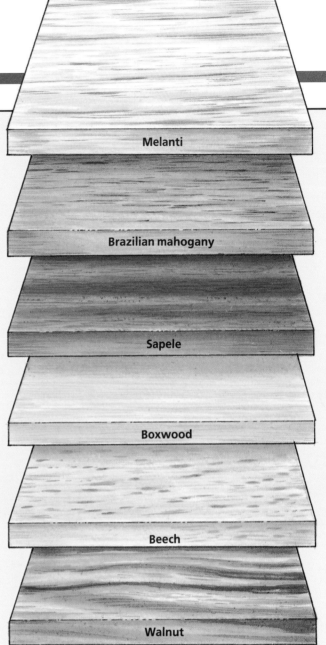

Melanti

Brazilian mahogany

Sapele

Boxwood

Beech

Walnut

## Types of wood

Woods like mahogany, sapele and melanti are from rainforest trees. Their felling damages the forest and the surrounding environment. In the future, there may be sustainable harvesting of these woods, perhaps from plantations. Until then, the use of tropical timber nearly always means the destruction of rainforests. For virtually all uses of tropical timber there are good alternatives, like walnut and beech from Europe and North America, and boxwood from the Mediterranean countries. These woods come from trees that are harvested in a more sustainable way than tropical rainforest timber.

# FACT FILE 2

## The water cycle

Nothing goes to waste in the rainforest. Most of the rain is taken up by the plants, used, and then released back into the atmosphere through their leaves. For the rest of the water, the roots of the trees in the rainforest act like a huge sponge, releasing water slowly into streams and rivers. The water that returns to the atmosphere falls again later as rain. Rain may be recycled up to 5 times as it passes from east to west across the Amazon, but deforestation stops this process and threatens to cause droughts.

Dead animals and plants decay quickly in the hot and humid conditions, their nutrients being taken up by the web of roots that grows close to the surface. Because everything is recycled quickly, a thick soil like that of cooler temperate forests does not form. This is why the soil can be easily washed away or lose its fertility under shifting cultivation when the forest is cleared.

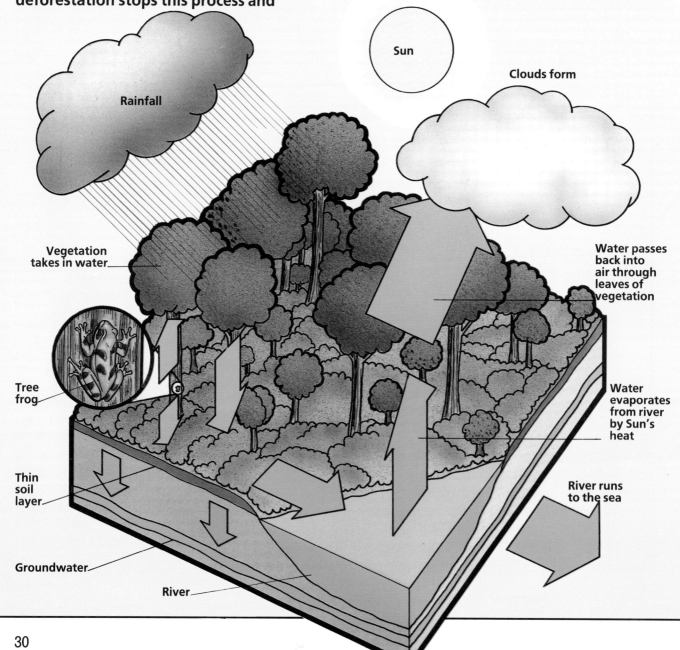

Sun

Rainfall

Clouds form

Vegetation takes in water

Water passes back into air through leaves of vegetation

Tree frog

Water evaporates from river by Sun's heat

Thin soil layer

River runs to the sea

Groundwater

River

# GLOSSARY

**Canopy** – the top layer of the rainforest. It is like the forest's roof, and is made up of the tops of the tallest trees. It makes first contact with sunlight and rain.

**Global warming** – the Earth's temperature varies naturally, warming and cooling over the ages. But when gases like carbon dioxide are put into the atmosphere as a result of, for example, burning coal, oil or gas for fuel, or burning rainforests to clear the land, they increase the greenhouse effect. This may be causing global warming, and could ultimately have dramatic effects on the climate worldwide.

**Greenhouse effect** – the natural warming effect of the Earth's atmosphere. Some gases, such as carbon dioxide, called "greenhouse gases", allow energy from the Sun to pass through to warm the Earth's surface, and then trap the heat as it rises back into the atmosphere. This keeps the atmosphere and the planet warm. It is known as the greenhouse effect and is one factor in making life on Earth possible.

**Rainforest** – a forest that grows where it is warm and rainy throughout the year.

**Ranching** – a type of farming where large areas of land are grazed by big herds of cattle. Many areas of rainforest have been cleared for cattle ranching. The cattle are bred for meat and milk.

**Shifted cultivation** – a kind of farming where people have been shifted into the forest because they are poor; there is nowhere else for them to go. They clear an area of forest, burn the trees and then grow crops. The ash from the trees helps fertilise the soil. But after several years the soil begins to lose its fertility and the farmers move on. The forest cannot recover because the nutrients have been used up, and devastation is left behind.

**Shifting cultivation** – the farming carried out by native peoples which does not harm the rainforest, though it looks similar at first glance to shifted cultivation. The people clear only small areas of land, they grow crops which belong in the rainforest, and they keep some vegetation over the ground all year. They move on before the land is completely exhausted and the forest recovers. Many years later the farmers may return and use the same patch of land, repeating the process.

# INDEX

**Photographic Credits:**
Cover and pages 21 top and 28 bottom left: Rex Features; pages 4-5, 6-7, 28 top left and top right: Planet Earth; pages 8, 10, 17 centre and bottom and 19: Topham; page 9 top: Ardea; pages 9 bottom, 12 right, 13, 14 left and right, 15 top right and bottom right, 17 top, 18, 21 bottom, 22 left, 24 and 25 bottom: Hutchison Photo Library; page 12 left: Bruce Coleman; page 15 top left: Christine Dodwell; page 25 top: Robert Harding.

PRINTED IN BELGIUM BY
proost
INTERNATIONAL BOOK PRODUCTION